IN A MINUTE

TAKE THE 60-SECOND CHALLENGE!

What can *you* do in a minute?

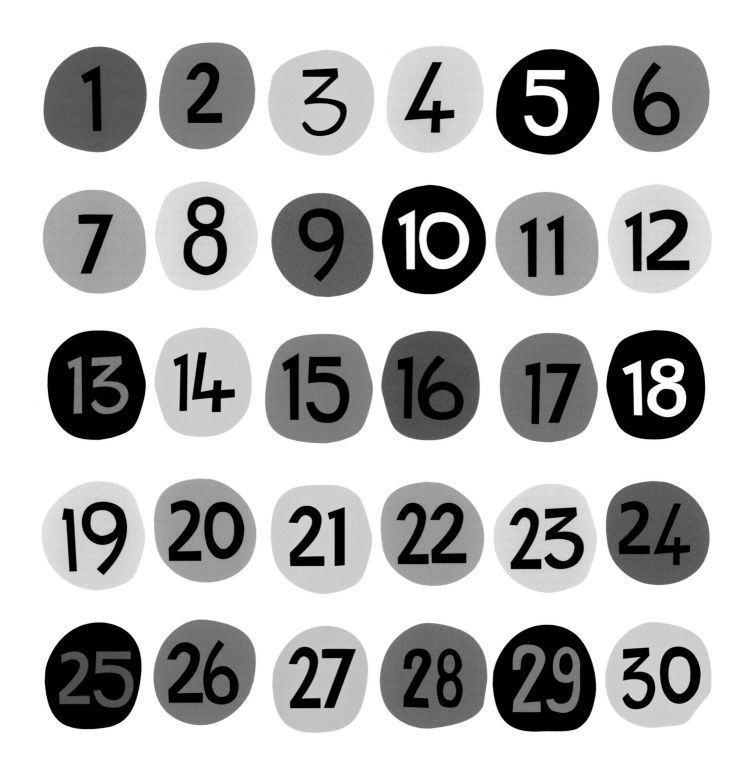

There are **60 seconds** in one minute.

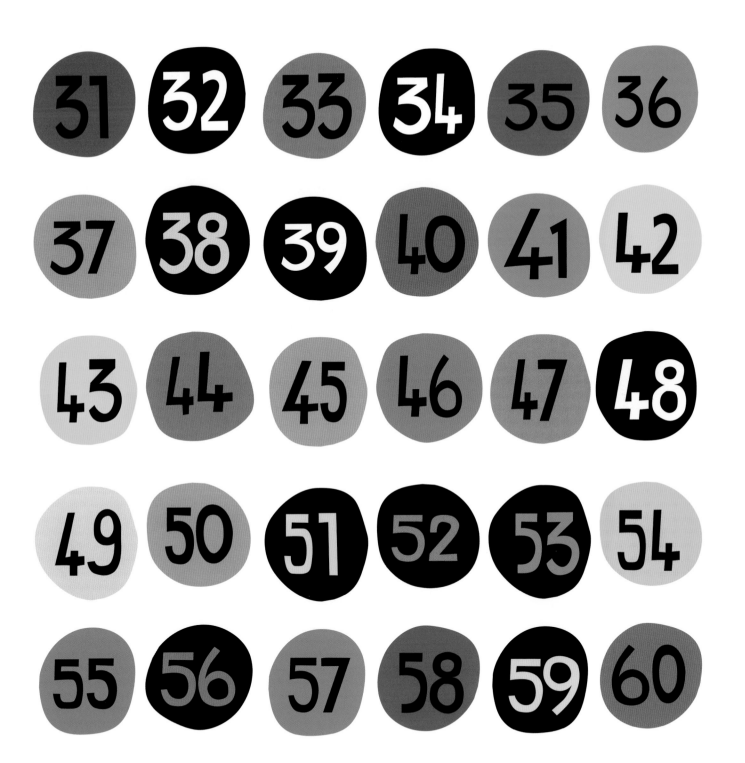

Can you **count** up to 60 in a minute?

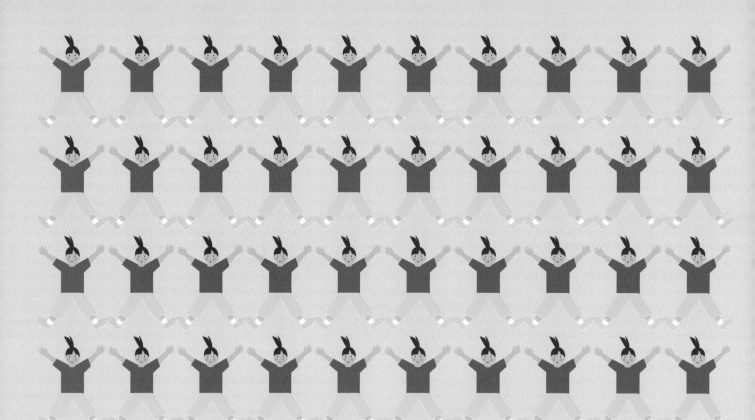

A winning star-jumper can **jump** 77 times in a minute.

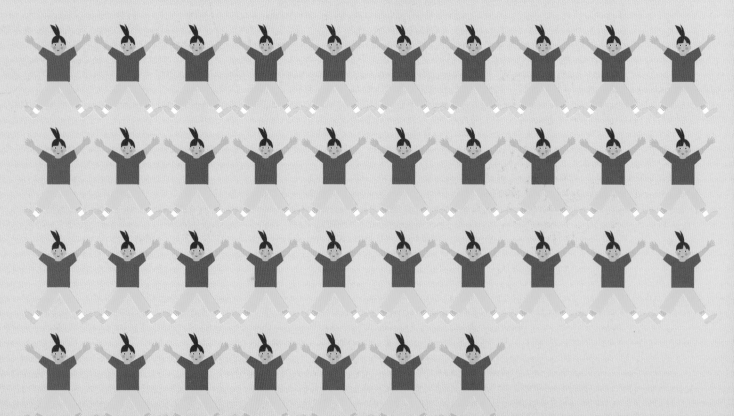

How many **star jumps**
can you do in a minute?

The number of beads on this page is the most anyone has **threaded** in a minute. There are 90 beads!

How many beads can you *thread* on to a string in a minute?

Think about what you
did yesterday.

How many things can you *remember* in a minute?

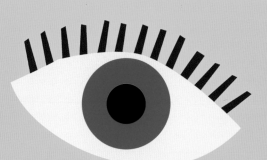

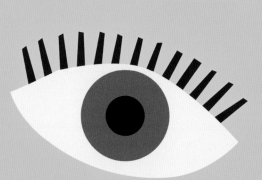

Blink non-stop.

Can you **blink** more than 20 times in a minute?

A woodpecker can **tap** 1,200 times
in a minute.

Tap your fingers as many
times as you can in a minute.

A butcher can *string*
78 sausages in a minute.

How many times can you **roll** like
a sausage in a minute?

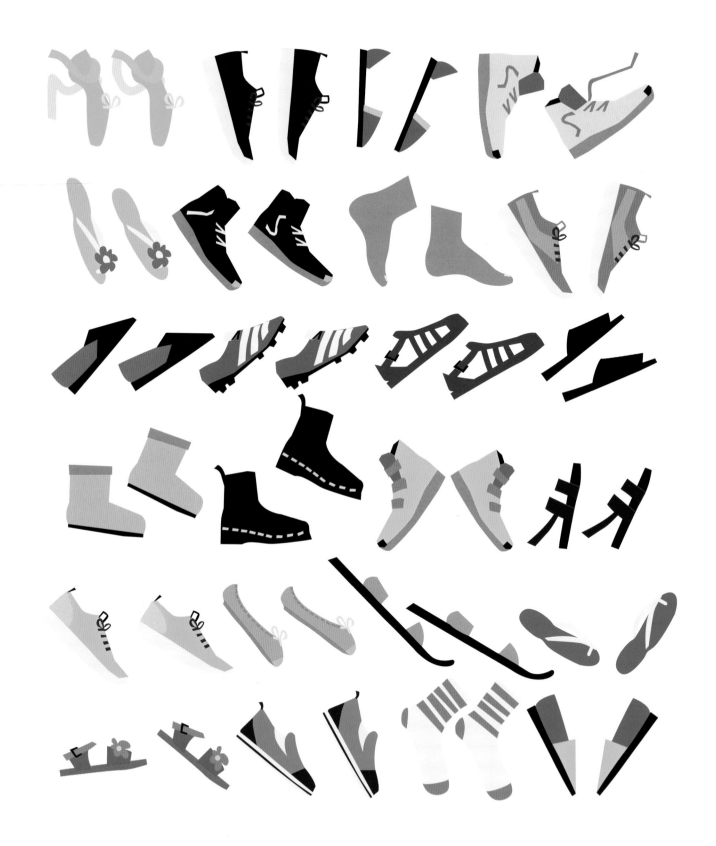

We can **move** our feet in all sorts of ways!

How many times can you **hop**
on just one foot in a minute?

A seahorse can *flap* its fin 2,100 times in a minute.

How many times can
you *flap* your arms
in a minute?

An anteater *slurps* up
24 ants in a minute.

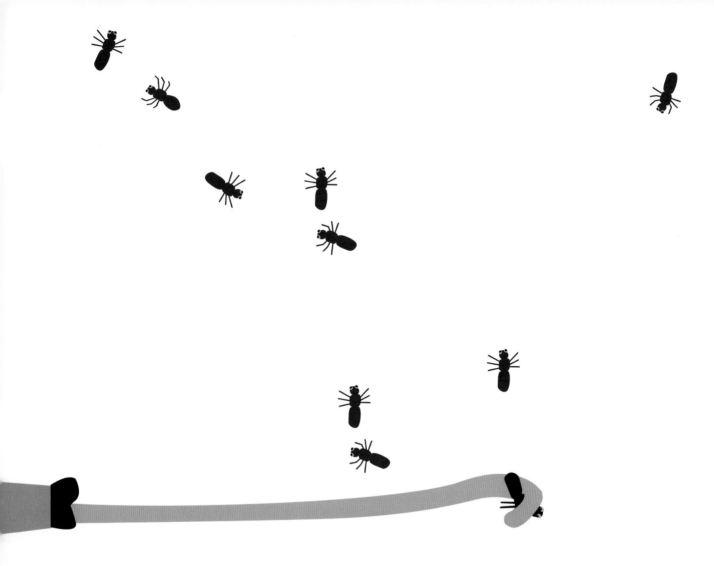

Stick your tongue in and out non-stop.
How many times can you do it in a minute?

A human heart **beats** up to 100 times a minute.

How many times does your own heart **beat** in a minute?

A chatterbox can **say** 170 words in a minute. Can you?

Two world-record jugglers can *catch*
11 clubs over 200 times in a minute.

How many balls can you *catch* in a minute?

Clap your hands as
many times as you can.

How many times
can you **clap** in
a minute?

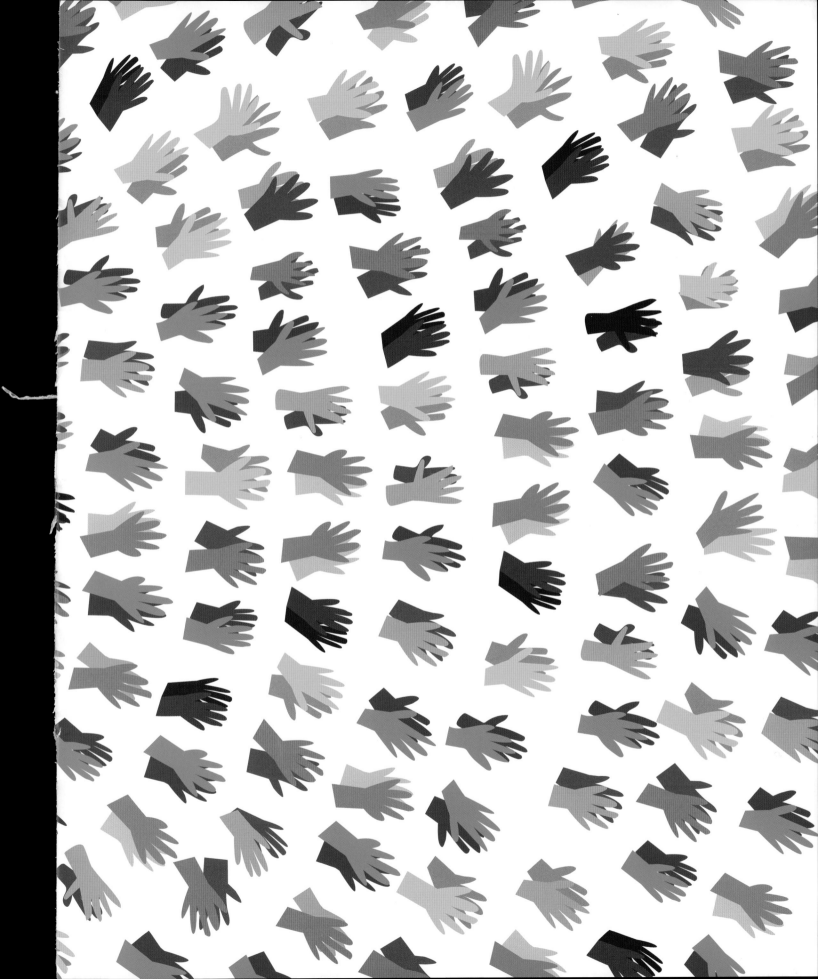

Try not to **do** anything at all for a minute.

Close your eyes . . . don't peek!

WELL DONE!

If you finished all the
60-second challenges in this book,
they will have taken you **15 minutes**.

Think about all the things you've done.
***What other amazing things
can you do in a minute?***

LADYBIRD BOOKS

UK | USA | Canada | Ireland | Australia
India | New Zealand | South Africa

Ladybird Books is part of the Penguin Random House group of companies
whose addresses can be found at global.penguinrandomhouse.com
www.penguin.co.uk   www.puffin.co.uk   www.ladybird.co.uk

Penguin
Random House
UK

First published 2019
001

Printed in China

A CIP catalogue record for this book is available from the British Library

ISBN: 978-0-241-31206-3

All correspondence to:
Ladybird Books, Penguin Random House Children's, 80 Strand, London WC2R 0RL

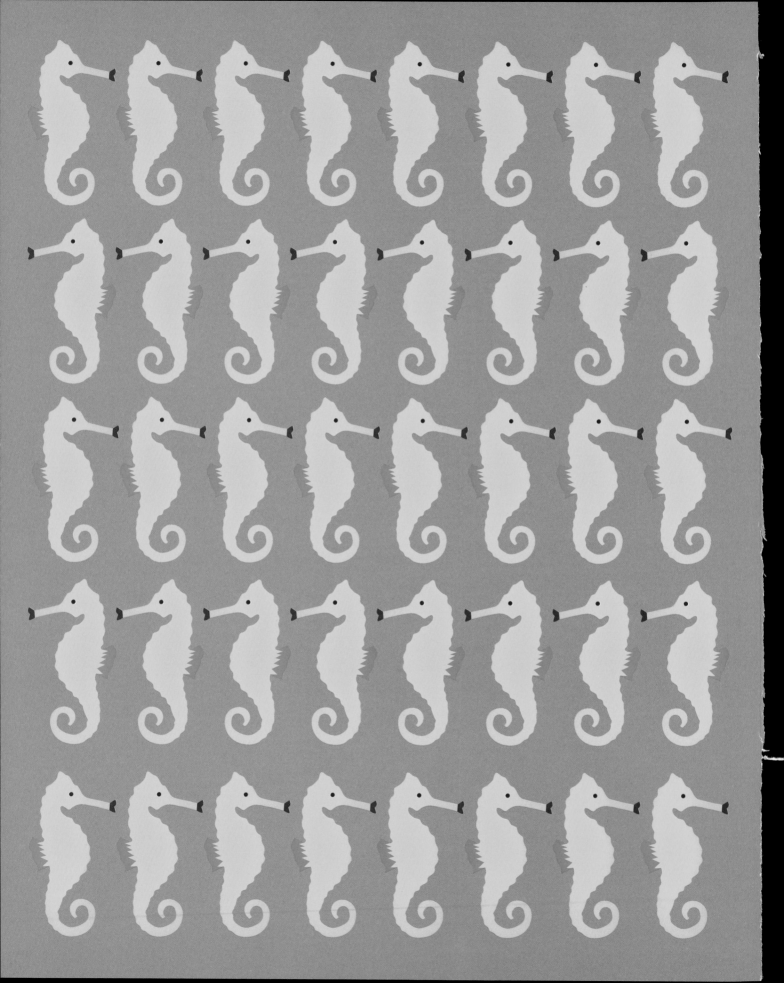